"The earth does not belong to us. We belong to the earth."

Chief Seattle, Native American leader

"Waste not, want not."

Proverb

"We won't have a society if we destroy the environment."

Margaret Mead, anthropologist

"When we try to pick out anything by itself, we find it hitched to everything else in the universe."

John Muir, naturalist

"Leave it as it is. You cannot improve on it; not a bit."

Theodore Roosevelt, American president

"A generation goes, and a generation comes, but the earth abides forever."

King James Bible, Ecclesiastes 1:4

For my environmental science students,
stewards who provide hope for our planet,
especially: Alissa Zimman, Kevin Vonck,
Laurel Schoenbohm, Robin Hillestad,
and Carrie LaRose.
—C.R.

# LET'S CELEBRATE EARTH DAY

By Connie and Peter Roop

Illustrated by Gwen Connelly

The Millbrook Press
Brookfield, Connecticut

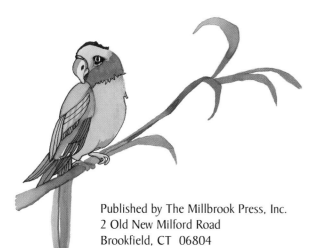

Published by The Millbrook Press, Inc.
2 Old New Milford Road
Brookfield, CT 06804
www.millbrookpress.com

Library of Congress Cataloging-in-Publication Data
Roop, Connie.
Let's celebrate earth day / by Connie and Peter Roop ;
illustrated by Gwen Connelly.
p.  cm.
ISBN 0-7613-1812-7 (lib. bdg.)   ISBN 0-7613-1690-6 (Pbk.)
!. Earth Day—Juvenile literature. 2. Environmentalism—United States—Juvenile
literature. 3. Environmental protection—United States—Juvenile literature. [I. Earth
Day. 2. Environmental protection. 3. Holidays.] I. Roop, Peter. II. Connelly, Gwen ill.
III. Title.
GE 195.5.R66 2001
363.7'0525—dc21  00-056623

Recycle! Reduce! Reuse! Bike! Walk! Ride the bus! Conserve water! Save energy! Endangered animals! Precious plants! Think globally, act locally! A multitude of messages encourage you to treat our earth with respect.

What day is it? Earth Day!

# What is Earth Day?

Earth Day
is a special day to celebrate
our planet. All across our continent
people do projects to help preserve and
protect the Earth's animals, plants, and habitats.
Some people clean up parks and playgrounds.
Others bike to school and work instead of riding
in a car. Some people pick up trash along
beaches or rivers. Others plant trees.
Schools have environmental fairs
and projects.

# When was the first Earth Day?

The first Earth Day was celebrated on April 22, 1970. Gaylord Nelson, a former U.S. senator from Wisconsin, decided that the best way to save our planet was to educate people on ways to protect and conserve. Have you ever heard the phrase: "If you're not part of the solution, you're part of the problem?" Gaylord Nelson decided he would be part of the solution, so he created Earth Day. And he didn't stop there. He worked to ban DDT, a dangerous pesticide, and phosphates in detergents, which polluted lakes and rivers. From Senator Nelson's one-person decision, our country now celebrates Earth Day in April.

# Did the first Earth Day make a difference?

In 1969 the Cuyahoga River near Lake Erie caught fire. How can water burn? If it is clean, it can't, but this river was badly polluted with oil, and oil can catch fire. This disaster caught the attention of the country. Something had to be done! The first Clean Air Act was passed in 1970. Cars had to be made more fuel efficient and the lead taken out of gasoline. In 1972 the first Clean Water Act became law. Businesses and communities had to stop dumping waste into our rivers and streams. In 1973 the Endangered Species Act protected plants and animals.

All of these laws have helped our Earth. Rivers are cleaner, cars pollute less, lead pollution in our air has been dramatically reduced, and many plants and animals have been brought back from the brink of extinction.

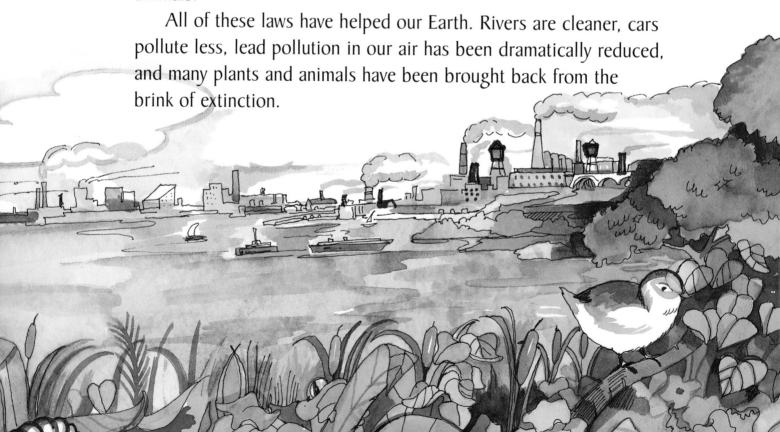

The four major oceans actually are one ocean separated by continents.

Each year Americans throw away 200 million tons of garbage. That's about 1,500 pounds (680 kilograms) for every man, woman, and child in the United States.

Earth is the only planet we know of with abundant life.

Each day thousands of trees in America are cut down.

Each night an area the size of Ohio is dragged clean of fish.

Learn about the habitat where you live. What plants and animals live there? What was your community like 20 years ago? 100 years ago? 200 years ago?

Ask your school to start a penny jar—at the end of the year adopt an endangered animal with the money collected.

Take a walk with your family—bring a garbage bag to pick up any trash along the way.

# What is an endangered species?

What do Florida panthers, whooping cranes, northern spotted owls, and green pitcher plants have in common? All are endangered species. Endangered species are plants and animals whose populations are so low they may become extinct. In the United States, the Carolina parakeet, the Arizona jaguar, and the Florida black wolf are some of the animals that have become extinct.

Once a plant or animal is extinct we will never see it again. It is gone forever. Early in the 1900s millions of passenger pigeons flew through our skies. People said it took hours for a flock to pass overhead. They were hunted for sport, and many people were surprised when, one day, there were no more passenger pigeons.

Today, with more than 6 billion people living on Earth, plants and animals are having a hard time finding a place to live. The loss of their habitat is the most serious threat to their survival.

The U.S. Fish & Wildlife Service collects information and determines what to put on the endangered species list. Some animals and plants are not yet endangered but are threatened. This is another list kept by the U.S. Fish & Wildlife Service. This means that unless we do something to save them, they, too, will become endangered and possibly extinct.

# Earth Day riddles

What is the dirtiest word on Earth?

Pollution!

How does the ocean say good-bye?

It waves!

What should you leave in a forest?

Your footprints!

What goes through the forest and never makes a sound?

A hiking trail!

# Should we protect every plant and animal?

No! There are some plants and animals that do more harm than good. These are alien, or invader, species. They are not from outer space. They are from Earth, but they are out of place!

Fire ants, whose ferocious sting feels like a burn, are not native to America. Yet billions of them have invaded the southern states. Originally from South America, fire ants have moved into North America and forced out other, gentler ants.

Purple loosestrife, a beautiful European plant, thrives in wetlands. But it takes over the wetlands, killing other plants of this habitat.

In 1988, European zebra mussels invaded the Great Lakes. They multiplied by the millions, taking over the homes of other creatures who cannot compete with them.

How do these invaders get here? Humans travel the Earth from the Arctic to Antarctica. Sometimes alien species hitch a ride on the bottoms of boats or in cargo shipments. Sometimes people bring plants and animals from one continent to another on purpose. When these invaders find a home they like, they are often the winners, and native plants and animals are the losers.

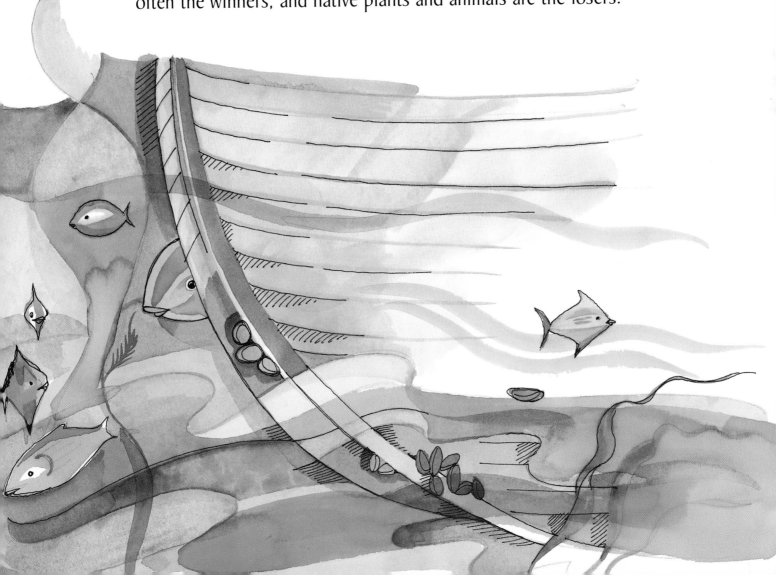

# Why does it matter where a plant or animal lives?

It matters because all life on Earth is interconnected. A native species that is getting crowded out may endanger something else that needs it to survive. As scientists study life on Earth, they are amazed by how many forms of life exist and how much they depend on one another. There are over 900 kinds of rain forest wasps, and each of these pollinate a specific fig plant. The wasps lay their eggs in the plant, and the young larva eat the fig nectar. Both the wasp and the fig plant depend on each other for survival.

Leaf-cutter ants have a partnership with fungus. They carry plant material back to their nests and chew up the leaves and flowers, which becomes food for the fungus. The leaf-cutter ants eat the fungus. Neither the fungus nor the ants can survive without one another.

Monarch butterflies migrate more than 1,000 miles (1,600 kilometers) to northern Mexico, spending the winter in one specific type of tree—the oyamel tree.

Bullhorn acacia trees depend upon the Pseudomyrmex ants to sting anything that touches it. In return, the ant lives in the tree's spines and eats the tree's nectar.

# Earth Day riddles

What has no feet, but can run?

Water!

Where do crocodiles keep their money?

In riverbanks!

What can roar, but doesn't have a mouth?

Fire!

# Are forest fires good or bad?

In 1988 a raging fire raced through our nation's oldest national park. Yellowstone was on fire! Fireballs in the treetops jumped streams and roads, carrying the fire farther into the park. By the time it was over, one third of the forest was gone. Most people believed this was a tragedy.

But was it? Fires are a necessary part of a forest's life. Scientists now know that forests need fires just like they need sunlight, water, and air. Too many nutrients released by decaying tree trunks and needles can actually poison the ground so young plants can't grow. Also, lodgepole pine, jack pine, and sequoia trees all need fire to open their cones. The heat melts a hard, waxy coating and releases the seeds inside. These seeds grow rapidly in the open, sunny areas created by fire. As the years pass, trees that like shade begin to grow.

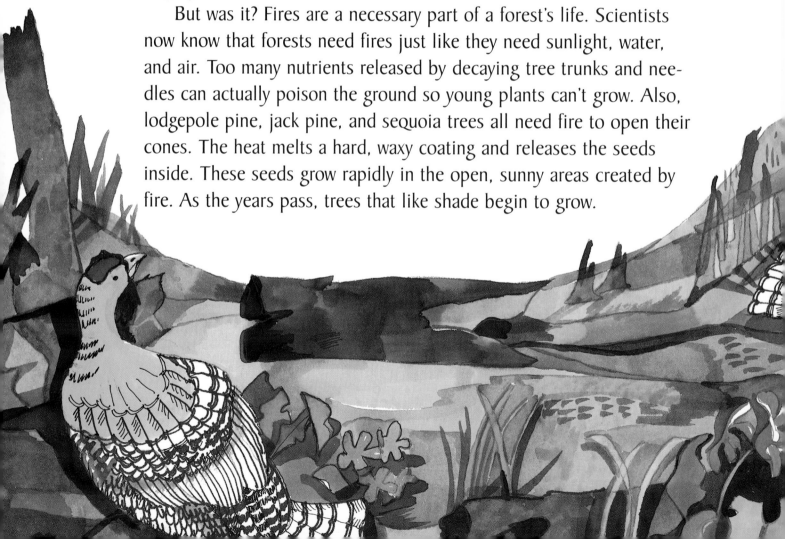

The dark earth created by a fire
absorbs more heat,
helping seeds sprout.

Mountain bluebirds,
grouse, and pine siskins
are animals that do well
after a fire.

Nutrients from burned
trees help enrich the
soil for new plants.

Fireweed, lupine, and
asters are plants that do
well after a fire.

# "Water, water, everywhere Nor any drop to drink."

Those lines were written by the poet Samuel Taylor Coleridge. Do you know how true they are? Even though 70 percent of the Earth is covered with water, almost all of it is salty! If all the water in the world were put into 100 cups, you could drink only 3 cups.

Most of the Earth's freshwater is trapped in the polar ice caps and in our atmosphere. Only 1 percent of the water on Earth is available to drink and use. Most of our freshwater comes from lakes, streams, rivers, and water underground. Much of this water is polluted.

Most of the freshwater we use is flushed down the toilet.

A water-saving toilet can save almost 10 gallons (38 liters) of water per person per day.

Wetlands help clean polluted water and prevent floods.

Don't leave the water running while you brush your teeth.

Don't throw out batteries, oil, paint, nail-polish bottles, or polish remover. Take them to your recycling center.

A leaky faucet wastes a huge amount of water—one drippy faucet lets 48 gallons (182 liters) a week go down the drain.

One person CAN make a difference!

Recycle

# Why is garbage a problem?

You eat a burger and fries at a fast-food restaurant. Walking out, you toss your wrappers, containers, straws, and napkins into the trash bin. Think about hundreds of thousands of people like you doing that all over the world. Uh-oh! Where does all this trash go?

Most trash is buried or burned. Both of these solutions cost money and cause pollution. What can you do? Buy less! Use less! Energy is saved and pollution is prevented when you recycle what you do buy.

Make your own wrapping paper by decorating paper grocery bags, and cut down on the trash you throw away.

During the weeks between Thanksgiving and New Year's Day, Americans throw away 1 million more tons of trash than usual.

Get things fixed instead of throwing them away.

Start a student petition to get recycling baskets into your cafeterias and paper recycling cans for the offices!

Paper    Glass    Garbage

# What is a fossil fuel?

Fossils fuels are energy sources that took millions of years to form. Oil, coal, and natural gas are fossil fuels. They come from the fossils of ancient animals and plants that decayed and released carbon, which changed into either oil, coal, or gas. We use these energy sources to power our cars, heat our homes, and make electricity.

When we burn fossil fuels we release the energy of the sun captured by living things millions of years ago. We also release carbon dioxide and nitrous oxide. These add to the Earth's air pollution. Wise use of these energy sources will save your family money, help these fuels last longer, and make the Earth a better place to live.

# Is there an energy source that's good for the Earth?

Wind energy, solar energy, and geothermal energy are all renewable resources. That means they can be used over and over.

For centuries, farmers have used windmills to pull water out of the ground. Today, windmill farms in Hawaii, California, and other states generate electricity.

Scientists are trying to create solar, or sun-powered, cars. Cars and trucks are our number one polluter and the biggest way we use fossil fuels.

Geothermal energy comes from hot water found in some places on Earth. Hot spots are found where melted rock from inside the Earth is closer to the Earth's surface. In Iceland, homes are heated with geothermal energy. In Gilmore, California, geo-thermal energy is used to make electricity for the town.

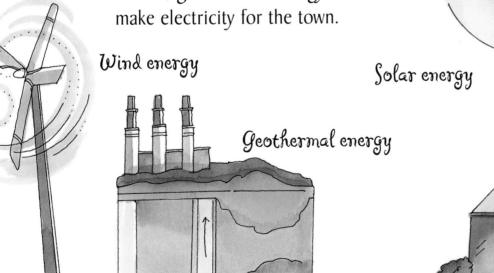

Wind energy

Geothermal energy

Solar energy

hot rock

# What is global warming?

If you leave your car in the sun with the windows closed it will get hotter in the car than it is outside. Just like the glass car windows, many gases in our atmosphere hold heat in. When we add certain gases to the atmosphere, more heat is trapped and the Earth becomes warmer. Carbon dioxide is one such gas. This and other gases come from cars and power plants.

Scientists call this the greenhouse effect, and the gases that cause it are called greenhouse gases. Because of these gases, the Earth is warming up. Scientists predict that severe storms and droughts may be a result of changes in the world's temperature.

# Recycle your lunch

You can recycle your food scraps to make rich soil. This is called composting. Do not use meat or dairy products, which make unpleasant smells.

## You will need:

two 2-liter soda bottles, one with a cap and one without
fruit and vegetable scraps such as apple cores, orange peels,
   banana peels, grape stems, lettuce and carrot tops, all cut into pieces
soil
water
clear, wide, strong packing tape
small square of cheesecloth
rubber band

1. Ask an adult to help you cut your bottles. The capped bottle gets cut in half around the middle. Cut the other bottle 2-3 inches (5-8 centimeters) from the bottom.
2. Using sharp scissors or a knife, ask an adult to cut air slits in the top parts of both bottles.
3. Construct your composting tower as shown.
4. Alternate layers of soil and food scraps.
5. Add just enough water to dampen your soil and food.
6. Seal up your tower with packing tape.

Look at your composting tower each week. Note how it changes. In several months you should have some rich soil to add to your indoor or outdoor plants!

# Ready for some good news?

The bald eagle, peregrine falcon, and northern sea otter are some of the animals that have been taken off the endangered species list. In the Pacific Northwest the largest remaining grove of ancient redwood trees, some of them more than 1,000 years old and 300 feet (91 meters) high, are now protected. The land was bought from a lumber company and will be preserved. In Toronto, Ontario, companies with offices in tall buildings have agreed to dim their lights when birds are migrating, so the birds won't get confused.

Everywhere around the world people
are waking up to the fact that one
person can make a difference.
Each one of us is responsible
for making the best choices for
the Earth every day, because
every day is Earth Day!

"Unless someone like you cares a whole awful lot, nothing is going to get better. It's not."

Dr. Seuss in The Lorax

"None of us can do all the things that will save the planet, but each of us can do some of them, and all of that will add up and be better than nothing."

Paula Danziger, author

"We are like butterflies who flutter for a day and think it is forever."

Carl Sagan, scientist

"There is not a sprig of grass that shoots uninteresting to me."

Thomas Jefferson, American president

"We need hours of aimless wandering . . . observing the mysterious world of ants and the canopy of treetops."

Maya Angelou, poet

"Those who dwell . . . among the beauties and mysteries of the earth are never alone or weary of life."

Rachel Carson, environmentalist and author